NATIONAL
GEOGRAPHIC
KiDS

A seed is the start

Melissa Stewart

NATIONAL GEOGRAPHIC
WASHINGTON, D.C.

For the students at
WEALTHY ELEMENTARY SCHOOL
in East Grand Rapids, Michigan,

who inspired me to write this book

Designer: Julide Dengel

Library of Congress Cataloging-in-Publication Data

Names: Stewart, Melissa, author.
Title: A seed is the start / by Melissa Stewart.
Description: Washington, D.C. : National Geographic Kids, 2018. | Includes
bibliographical references.
Identifiers: LCCN 2017010960| ISBN 9781426329777 (hardcover : alk. paper) |
ISBN 9781426329784 (hardcover : alk. paper)
Subjects: LCSH: Seeds--Juvenile literature. | Plants--Juvenile literature.
Classification: LCC QK661 .S7436 2018 | DDC 581.4/67--dc23
LC record available at https://lccn.loc.gov/2017010960

Printed in Hong Kong
17/THK/1

Words to Know

Understanding what they mean will help you as you read the book.

Berry: A small, round, brightly colored fruit. It usually has many tiny seeds.

Burr: A rough, prickly covering that surrounds some seeds or fruits

Fruit: The part of a plant that holds seeds

Nut: A fruit with a hard shell. Most nuts have just one seed.

Seed: The part of a plant that can grow into a new plant. It forms inside a fruit.

Seedpod: A fruit that holds many seeds. When it is ripe, it splits open and releases the seeds inside.

A **seed** is the start of a new plant life. Bury it in soil, and watch it **grow, grow, grow.**

What happens when you plant a **corn seed** ?

First, the seed coat splits open.

Then a root pushes down into the soil. It soaks up water and minerals.

Next, a shoot pokes up out of the soil.

The shoot stretches toward the sun.

The corn plant's first leaves spread open. They collect sunlight, so the plant can make food and keep on growing.

Plants grow best when they have their own space. That's why seeds have many ways of **traveling** to new places.

When a seed sprouts under its parent plant, it may have trouble growing. The young plant may not get enough sunlight to make food.

When many seeds sprout close together, young plants struggle to survive. Some may not get the water and minerals they need.

Seeds fly.

Dozens of seeds form inside a milkweed seedpod. When the seeds are full-grown, the pod bursts open. Then the wind whisks the seeds away.

How do milkweed seeds fly through the air? Each seed has dozens of light, silky hairs. The wind lifts the hairs up, up, up. It carries the seed through the sky.

Each dandelion seed grows inside a hard brown nut.

The nut's long stem is attached to a clump of silky hairs. The wind can blow a dandelion seed up to 500 miles (805 km) away.

Seeds spin and glide.

When this red maple fruit is ripe, its stem will break. The fruit will spin and spin, like the blades on a helicopter. It may travel the length of two American football fields.

After the fruit lands, its tough coat slowly breaks down. Then its two seeds can grow into new trees.

When a gourd cracks open, hundreds of seeds take flight. They glide through the trees. After a seed lands, its wings slowly rot away. Then a new vine sprouts.

Look at these Asian climbing gourds!
These fruits are the size of basketballs. They grow on vines in the rain forests of Southeast Asia.

Seeds tumble and

As a Russian thistle's fruits grow, the plant dries out. Its leaves turn brown. Then its stem breaks away from the roots.

When the wind blows, the plant rolls across the land. People call it a tumbleweed. A tumbling tumbleweed scatters its 250,000 seeds far and wide.

spill.

After the red petals fall away, the fruit grows larger. Then it dries out.

While a poppy blooms, a small, round fruit forms inside the flower.

When the stem sways in the wind, seeds spill out of holes at the top of the dried poppy fruit. If they land in dark, damp soil, they will grow into new plants.

Seeds splash.

Marsh marigolds grow near ponds and streams, swamps and marshes. After they bloom, seedpods form. When the seeds are ready, the pods split open.

During summer storms, raindrops strike the seeds and knock them into the water. *Splash!* The seeds float to new places.

Living stones grow in dry, sandy deserts. It's easy to mistake them for rocks—until their flowers bloom.

When the seedpods are ripe, they wait for rain. When it finally falls, raindrops splash the seedpods. *Pop!* The seedpods burst open. Water surges over the seeds and washes them away.

Seeds float.

Have you seen yellow irises growing in gardens? A lot of people love these flowers. But irises grow naturally in wet places, like this lake in British Columbia, Canada.

After an iris flower withers away, a seedpod forms. When it's ripe, it breaks open. The seeds drop into the water and float away.

Imagine a snowstorm of seeds. That's what it looks like when hundreds of cottonwood fruits split open at the same time.

Cottonwood trees grow near rivers and lakes. Their tiny, fluff-covered seeds land on the water and travel to new places.

Seeds drift.

The red hamburger bean vine grows in the rain forests of Central and South America. When the seedpods are ripe, they split open. Two one-inch (2.5-cm) seeds fall out.

How did the red hamburger bean vine get its name? From the look of its seeds! When rain falls, the seeds are washed into streams and rivers. They're swept into the ocean and can drift for thousands of miles.

People plant coconut palms in all kinds of places.
But they grow naturally on warm, sandy beaches. Each coconut fruit has one seed inside.

When the fruit is ripe, it falls. Down, down, down. It might land in the ocean. Or it might hit the ground and then roll into the sea.

Air pockets inside a coconut fruit help it stay afloat. It can drift on the currents for days or weeks or months. The seed inside the coconut fruit shown here started to sprout during its journey.

Seeds pop.

Look at these lovely little flowers.
You'd never guess how a Himalayan balsam sends its seeds into the world.

When a breeze blows or an animal passes by ... *Pop!*
The seeds burst out in every direction. They may blast up to 15 feet (4.6 m) away.

A sandbox tree fruit looks like a small pumpkin. But when the fruit is ripe, it explodes into thin pieces. *Bang!* The sound rings out through the rain forest.

Each piece contains a large, flat seed. It blasts through the air at speeds of 150 miles an hour (241 km/h). The seeds may travel the length of seven school buses parked end to end.

seeds hop and

Wild oat plants often pop up in wheat fields.
Why do their seeds have a long, bent tail? So they can move away from their parent plant.

See how part of the seed's tail is twisted? As it winds and unwinds, pressure builds up along the straight tip. Finally, the tip springs forward, and the seed jumps. Over time, it hop, hop, hops across the ground.

creep.

Look at the lovely blue cornflowers!

As their petals dry out, fruits form inside the flower. Then the fruits fall to the ground.

Each fruit has a seed at one end. There is a tuft of stiff bristles at the other end.

When the air is dry, the bristles shrink. On humid days, the bristles swell. Thanks to these tiny movements, the seed slowly creeps across the ground.

23

seeds hook and cling.

See the bulging green fruit below this burdock's pink flower? It is surrounded by a spiky covering called a burr. After the flower fades, the fruit dries out and its burr turns brown.

A burdock's burr has lots of tiny hooks. When an animal passes by, the hooks get caught in its fur. Then the animal carries the fruit to a new place.

When the fruit falls to the ground, it splits open. Then seeds spill onto the ground.

Queen Anne's lace grows in fields and along roads. As its fruits ripen, they curl up to form a ball. Each fruit has two seeds on the inside. It has dozens of sticky spines on the outside.

When an animal passes by, the fruits cling to its coat. The animal may carry the seeds for miles.

Seeds ride inside.

This bird, called a fieldfare, can't resist eating a tasty rowan berry. As it flies from place to place, the seeds ride inside its body—until the bird poops. Then the seeds land in a new spot.

In warm parts of the world, many bats eat fruit. Their bodies break down the soft, sweet pulp. But not the hard, tough seeds. Each time the bats poop, they spread the seeds to new places.

Because berries are small, a deer doesn't have to chew them. That means the seeds stay safe as they pass through the animal's body. A few days later, the deer poops out the seeds far away from the parent plant.

Seeds ride outside, too.

When ants find a bloodroot seed, they don't eat it. They pick it up and take it for a ride. Where are they headed? Back to their nest.

The ants share the tasty food packet on top of the seed. Then they dump the seed in their waste pile. That's good news for the seed. It's surrounded by rich soil full of rotting material. What a perfect place to grow!

Some people collect the seeds of plants they like. They take the seeds home and grow them in their yards.

Other people buy packets of seeds at a store. Then they plant the seeds in a garden.

In the autumn, gray squirrels collect hundreds of nuts and seeds. They carry the food to safe spots. Then they bury it.

During the winter, squirrels eat some of the nuts and seeds. But they forget about others. In the spring, the leftover seeds sprout. They grow into new plants.

If a seed lands in a good spot, **it sprouts.**

When an apple seed sprouts, the tiny new plant stretches toward the sun.

As time passes, the plant grows larger and larger. Now it looks like a young tree.

Then it grows into a plant that makes more **seeds.**

When the tree is old enough, it begins to produce flowers.

Then fruits develop with new seeds inside.

An apple tree can produce hundreds of apples each year. And each apple can have up to 10 seeds. How many new seeds can an apple tree make in just one year? Thousands.

INDEX

SELECTED SOURCES

"Burdock," and "Queen Anne's Lace," Edible Wild Food.
Available online at ediblewildfood.com.

Burns, Diane L. *Berries, Nuts, and Seeds.* Gareth Stevens, 2000.

"Fruit and Seed Dispersal." Vanderbilt University Bioimages.
Available online at bioimages.vanderbilt.edu/pages/fruit-seed-dispersal.htm.

Kesseler, Rob, and Wolfgang Stuppy. *Seeds.* Firefly Books, 2006.

Kueny, Meredith. "Seed Dispersal." Cornell University's Naturalist Outreach. Available online at calscomm.cals.cornell.edu/naturalist/Naturalist-Outreach-Seed-dispersal.pdf.

Parolin, Pia. "Ombrohydrochory: Rain-operated Seed Dispersal in Plants." *Flora* (October 12, 2016), 511–518.

Stewart, Melissa. Personal observations recorded in nature journals, 1989-present.

Wiest, Betty. "Samaras and Other Forms of Seed Dispersal." *NorthJersey.com*, June 12, 2015.
Available online at northjersey.com/community-news/recreation/samaras-and-other-forms-of-seed-dispersal-1.1354655.

FOR MORE INFORMATION

BOOKS

Aston, Dianna Hutts. *A Seed Is Sleepy.* Chronicle Books, 2007.

Esbaum, Jill. *Seed, Sprout, Pumpkin, Pie.* National Geographic Kids Books, 2009.

Galbraith, Kathryn O. *Planting the Wild Garden.* Peachtree Publishers, 2011.

Macken, JoAnn Early. *Flip, Float, Fly: Seeds on the Move.* Holiday House, 2008.

Rattini, Kristin Baird. *Seed to Plant.* National Geographic Kids Books, 2014.

ONLINE

BBC Nature Wildlife: Seed Aviation
bbc.co.uk/nature/adaptations/Seed_dispersal#p00lxw4t.